ENJOY THE RIDE!

The A-Z Handbook for Life

ENJOY THE RIDE!

Robert Osbourne

Copyright © 2019 Robert Osbourne

The moral right of the author has been asserted.

Apart from any fair dealing for the purposes of research or private study, or criticism or review, as permitted under the Copyright, Designs and Patents Act 1988, this publication may only be reproduced, stored or transmitted, in any form or by any means, with the prior permission in writing of the publishers, or in the case of reprographic reproduction in accordance with the terms of licences issued by the Copyright Licensing Agency. Enquiries concerning reproduction outside those terms should be sent to the publishers.

Matador
9 Priory Business Park,
Wistow Road, Kibworth Beauchamp,
Leicestershire, LE8 0RX
Tel: 0116 279 2299
Email: books@troubador.co.uk
Web: www.troubador.co.uk/matador
Twitter: @matadorbooks

ISBN 978 1838591 069

British Library Cataloguing in Publication Data.
A catalogue record for this book is available from the British Library.

Printed on FSC accredited paper
Printed and bound in Great Britain by 4edge Limited
Typeset in 11pt Minion Pro by Troubador Publishing Ltd, Leicester, UK

Matador is an imprint of Troubador Publishing Ltd

*This book is dedicated to my special ones,
K, R and M, who do so much to make my own
journey through life such an enjoyable one*

CONTENTS

Introduction	ix
Letter to my children	xi
Ambition	3
Broadmindedness	9
Creativity	15
Determination	21
Education	27
Family (and friends)	33
Gratitude	39
Hope	45
Interests	51
Joy	57
Kindness	63

Love	69
Money	75
Nature	81
Originality	87
Preparation	93
Questioning	99
Reflection	105
Sensitivity	111
Time	117
Understanding	123
Valour	129
Work	135
Xmas	141
Youthfulness	147
Zest	153

INTRODUCTION

This has been a *really* fulfilling project that I have for many a year had the intention of embarking upon. There is so much to life and those of us who are now well into middle age have, through our own life experiences, created little pockets of wisdom that we cannot help but want to pass on. I am a teacher by profession and that is maybe where it all comes from. What we teachers do day in, day out is precisely that and yet I have come to realise that a lot of what I have seen, heard, enjoyed, endured and even suffered over the years has not really been properly shared with my own children. What I have learnt I really want to share with them and let them see the inner me, let them know how I feel about so many aspects of life that we never address in our conversations, never mind how in-depth they are. I have decided that the only way I can do this halfway adequately is to write it all down, to share it with them on paper, so this is the result.

I have chosen this format as I seem to be able to include what I want to say quite conveniently under those alphabetical headings and it limits the number to a nicely manageable twenty-six, which I hope will make it tolerably readable for you all and it may even start a trend of parents writing such messages to their children; who knows? What I can say is that after completing it, I am glad. It has given me the opportunity to tell my children lots of things without interruption, without ribbing, without comment! That's great in itself! It also allows me to leave something of myself for my children when I am long gone and it gives me a real sense of pleasure and satisfaction to know that I have done this for them and that through doing so, they may well know me better. Those of you who have had children will know how they enrich our lives and give us such joy and pride, and most of us would agree that they are the best things we ever did, but how often do we tell them that? How do we begin to do so when they are adults or nearly so? Well, this is how. We write it down so it's there in black and white. They are special and we want them to know, so this is a means that makes it clear. I know that this is a very much a personal message to my own children, but I trust that you will find it interesting, relevant and readable nonetheless. As I say, its creation has given me immense pleasure. Enjoy the read!

LETTER TO MY CHILDREN

Dear kids,

This is a book that I have written for you, and I have loved the process of bringing it to life and of putting on paper things that, for many reasons, I cannot express to you in any other way. For me, it is a message of love and support that I hope that you will carry with you. I have no idea how you will react to it, but I do hope that you will enjoy reading it and will understand why I have chosen to write it. It is my first book of any description and it is something that I have had in mind for a while without previously having had enough time to commit to the project in a way that would do it justice. As I have prevaricated, similar books have appeared by some very able writers, and these have been excellent pieces of work, but I have decided that this quite selective A–Z format suits me best and covers the key bases, and I have finally taken the plunge. I hope you like it!

The passage of the years teaches you that there are some things in life that are important and there are plenty more that are not and I have very much focused on the former. I want you to make the most of life and achieve everything that you want to, and I want to help you as much as I can. Life is a real sea of waves and troughs and it's as though we are small boats on these waves being buffeted by the winds and currents and facing all kinds of situations where careful navigation is required. However, I hope that there will also be plenty of calm seas along the way when you are able to relax and enjoy the view, so to speak. My aim here is to give you as much help as possible to ensure that you end up sailing calmer, less dangerous waters and are therefore able to make the most of this wonderful journey you have embarked upon.

I sometimes look back on my life whilst sipping a cappuccino and reflect on how I have contrived to spend my days thus far. Like most people, I have happy memories aplenty, as well as more than a few regrets. I would maybe like to turn the clock back to rectify a few things, but life does not allow that. You have one attempt at it and that's it, and the more help and support you have when you start making important decisions, then the less likely you are to regret things that you have done. All three of you are sensible people who have the right approach to life in so many ways and your mother and I should have no concern about letting you set off on life's journey, but we are parents and we will always worry, and you will do the same with your own children, believe me. It goes with the territory, as they say. Parents cannot help it; they cannot truly let go and the reason for that is simple: you are what life is all about. You are the best thing we ever did and ever will do and we cannot begin to describe what you mean to us and how you add so much colour and joy to our lives. For you we will always be grateful and we will always be there to love and support you in every way we can – and we mean, *always*.

Dad (and Mum) xxx

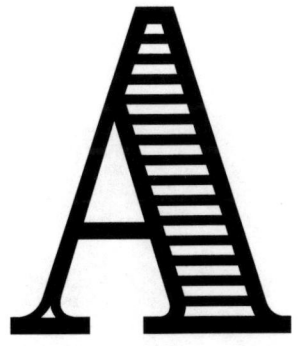

is for

AMBITION

"The Gospel of Getting On."

George Bernard Shaw (*Mrs Warren's Profession*, 1898)

AMBITION

I will begin by saying that having ambition helps in life. Although this is not something that all young people need to possess, I have come to believe that when you are older and look back over your life, you really need to feel that you have given it your best shot and have aimed as high as you can, or to have tried to achieve something in whichever field you have chosen to enter. In the words of Robert Browning:

"Ah, but a man's reach should exceed his grasp,
Or what's a heaven for?"

As a youngster I had no real career ambitions. I flirted with the idea of teaching or working in personnel in some way, but beyond getting to a good university to study languages, I had no other driving force. Saying that, I worked jolly hard and sacrificed much potential teenage fun to achieve that small ambition and thankfully was successful. It does make me wonder, though, what would have happened if I had entertained the idea of a career plan or had simply spent the time thinking about what areas might have suited me. In those days, that was rare. It was more common to drift into employment and then see where life took you. That's nice in some ways, but when you think how much of your life is dominated by the workplace and how it defines you, it does pay to give it a little thought at your stage of life.

I have to say, though, that at an early age, I decided that I would not let money drive my career decisions. Whilst that seemed very virtuous at the time (and note that I stuck to this position by leaving accountancy and going into teaching), I'm not sure that I could so easily take that decision these days with the advent of students paying for tuition fees, etc. Teaching has been great, as it's a job in which you help to shape so many lives and that is wonderfully valuable and satisfying. However, I do hope that in years to come, students are able to be free of such financial burdens and can experience university and their early working life with the freedom and joy that my generation and those before us were able to do.

Hopefully when you get a job, opportunities for promotion should be there and if so, take them and aim to be the best that you can be, whilst at the same time making sure that you can do the job. There's nothing worse than gaining that promotion and finding that the new post is that much trickier than you had anticipated.

Ambition does appear in other guises too and these are, in my view, much more satisfying. Think about it in terms of your friends, family and living environment. Ambition equates to having plans there, too, and as these are so close to you, they are that much more enjoyable to plan and experience. An ambition of mine, I'm not afraid to say it, was to be a family man. I looked forward to being married and having a family one day and here I am, writing this piece to you, to let you know how delighted I am at having achieved that and how much joy and pleasure that particular ambition has brought me. And ambitions should do precisely that – they should bring you immense pleasure. That is why they are what they are as you are aiming to arrive at a place where you will feel great. When you have a house, for example, it is quite natural to want to improve it and develop it in a way that makes you feel proud and comfortable, and that's quite a target too, I can tell you! I can't say that I have really been ambitious enough in that direction, but I can already tell that you will all be quite different – hooray!

An ambition that I hope you will all have is to experience the world and what's out there. Yes, it seems to be an increasingly dangerous place and as parents, we worry how the world will be for you and your own children, but at the same time, it is fascinating and one of my own remaining ambitions is to travel more and learn more about different countries and peoples. Don't be afraid to travel, as it really does open your eyes to so much and broadens the mind. We have done our best in your lifetimes to travel to different parts of Europe – yes, to find the hot sun and fine food, but also to stimulate your interest in cultures other than you own. Saying that though, do not forget what the UK has to offer. There is so much here to explore – so much history, so many lovely towns, villages, lakes, hills and mountains. Bill Bryson has made a living out of it, so there really is so much to see and do. Definitely make it an ambition to get to know your own country and its delights too.

So you see, ambition comes in many forms and there is a crossover here with other aspects of living that I will cover later in this book, but my message really is to have a good measure of it, extending to different areas of your lives. You do not always have to fulfil initial ambitions and sometimes circumstances are such that you have to alter plans, but simply replace them with others and, above all, appreciate the journey as it always makes arriving there that much more special. It would be great if you could one day look back and say that the world is now a better place for you having been in it.

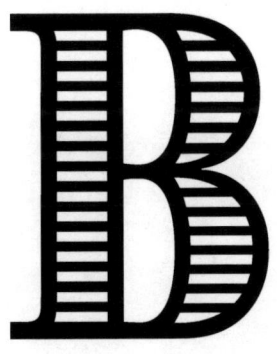

is for

BROADMINDEDNESS

"The superior man is broadmined."

Confucius (*Analects,* ch2 v14)

BROADMINDEDNESS

When I was a small boy of six or seven years of age, a very pleasant, normally most genial member of the teaching staff, gathered the class together in the school hall and began talking about race and colour. He then became very angry as he maintained that we should never treat people differently because of the colour of their skin. He emphasised strongly that we are all alike. Now I remember that talk even today, forty-five years later, and I remember it not only because the normally mild-mannered teacher raised his voice and shouted at us, but also because we were so surprised that there was even a discussion about it. We naturally saw no difference whatsoever. There were certainly some black and Asian children in the school, but we saw no issue with that – there was no natural inclination on our part to see them as different, as being apart in some way. As this was the 1970s, I soon came to realise – sadly through the very evident level of prejudice on television – why he had found it so important to deliver that talk to us when we were so small. Through some members of an older generation represented in the programmes, attitudes that might be seen as racist were certainly present on occasion. As so many people watched a smaller number of television programmes in those days and discussed them at work and, of course, at school, it was so easy for youngsters to adopt the views that were represented. Thankfully, it really was a minority, and we live in much more enlightened times and people rightly abhor such views. Thankfully too, your generation is even better than ours and has a real nose for prejudice and injustice, so this can be a pretty short chapter!

Now, this may well be the case in the UK, but in other parts of the world, intolerance and old-fashioned views still predominate. I have already encouraged you to travel – and there are many benefits of doing so – but sadly you will encounter prejudice in some forms and attitudes contradictory to your own, and whilst it may be hard to alter those, you can still remain true to your own values and perceptions of the world. However, other cultures have much to teach us too. We are certainly not perfect here in the UK. We have to appreciate the merits of other nations and how they live their lives – I'm sure we agree that other countries often do things better and people are happier, so we can learn from them too.

Being politically broadminded is a trickier one! I am never going to suggest where you should align yourselves politically, suffice to say that it is important to appreciate that in our democracy everyone has a voice and the right to be listened to, whether their views are agreeable to people or not. We must respect people's right to their views, and being broadminded is precisely that.

So what is my message on broadmindedness? Well, it's simply this. I have much faith in your generation and in your attitudes and level of understanding of different cultures and political viewpoints. In essence, as you grow older you are tempted to become less broadminded as you become more certain of your views and your levels of tolerance of others – guard against this. The world is a wonderful place and there is space enough for all as long as we are kind and loving to each other and want the best for humanity.

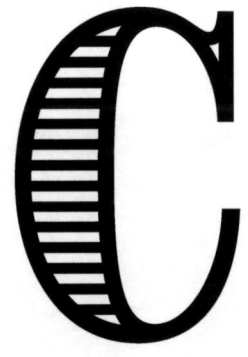

is for

CREATIVITY

"Odd how the creative power at once brings the whole universe to order."

Virginia Woolf

CREATIVITY

This is an important one, and something that I have always championed. Without creativity, where would we be? Where would we find our beautiful artwork, architecture, music, new inventions, literature and so on? It involves setting your imagination free and letting it take you where it can. However, you need to let it flourish, you need to give it time and eventually it may produce something truly amazing. So, whenever you can, be creative, or rather, keep being creative. When you were all small, you were so keen to draw, paint, write, build and generally produce things of beauty using all your acquired skills and best efforts. And how proud you were of what you achieved and how delighted we were to have your offerings, which you so often produced just for us. We have kept so many of them and it's always a pleasure to unearth them now and then and be reminded of those days! However, your creativity has not disappeared since then – far from it! It has just been channelled into different things, such as school artwork, projects, musical pieces, poems, short stories and essays. The only difference is that for the most part, you are requested to do these things rather than having some spare time to indulge a passion, as your first creative efforts certainly revealed. Your aim should be to try to put aside time again as adults to reignite those passions and see where they take you.

As you have developed into young adults, you have, as teenagers do, allowed yourselves to become more self-critical, and that is hard to shake off. I am certainly in the same boat myself, which is why I have not produced anything worthy of note despite the odd assembly. Saying that, it could be argued that there is much creativity in teaching, as you have to craft lessons, and that's certainly true, but the creativity I am talking about is the type that exists without pressure, without expectation and without fear of judgement or ridicule. That's the creativity that's really fun.

There is, of course, one area in which you are all constantly exploring your creativity and excelling, and that is in your cooking and baking. I have no skills whatsoever in that area, but you have all been inspired by your mother to produce cakes and meals of great variety and, frankly, quite superb appearance and taste and they are getting better and better! I'm so delighted that you made use of that freedom that we happily offered you to use the kitchen how and when you wanted to produce whatever took your fancy. That's definitely real creativity at work and you must always give that creative urge free rein whenever you have that opportunity. I know that it will not be easy, as work, household chores and general life pressures eat into free time like hostile forces and it can be hard to find time, energy and real inclination to push yourself to reveal and shape your creativity, but always try – if not immediately, then here and there as the years pass. And good luck with whatever you choose to do.

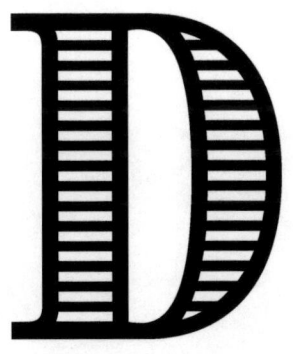

is for

DETERMINATION

"Yes We Can."

Barack Obama

DETERMINATION

This is a great one, as there is nothing more satisfying than giving something all you've got and being able to reach your goal. The more effort you put in, the more pleasurable it is when you get there. It goes hand in hand with persistence, and a great example of this was the nineteenth-century US president, Abraham Lincoln. He was born into poverty and faced defeat and loss throughout his life, including the death of his first love, losing eight elections, failing in business and suffering a nervous breakdown. He could have given up many times and because his resolute determination prevented him from doing so, he became one of the greatest presidents in US history. His ability to keep going despite his setbacks gave him the strength to be exceptional when he finally achieved his goal. The American motor entrepreneur Henry Ford saw 'failure as an opportunity to begin again, but this time more intelligently' and, indeed, he lost his inventors a lot of money before he finally made it with his Ford Motor Company. The film director Steven Spielberg was rejected by the USC School of Cinematic Arts on account of poor grades, switched to a degree in English and ended up teaching himself to direct. Closer to home, Richard Branson failed many of his exams and was considered to be a poor student, but through grit and determination, he eventually founded a magazine, a recording studio and then the airline Virgin Atlantic and a lot more besides. He is now one of the wealthiest people in the UK.

However, like ambition, determination can reap its benefits in all areas of life and that's why I have given it an entry here. I have spent four years (!) trying to get the electricity company to move overhead powerlines from over our garden. I have had to engage legal experts and chase up all manner of employees again and again to get things moving, as not all parties were as willing as me to get things done, but finally, we are at the point of success; what an effort it's been. The champagne corks will definitely be popping when it's all over, believe me! I won't deny that writing this book needs buckets of determination. As I write now, it's the summer holidays, it's lovely outside, you are all happily talking and laughing in the kitchen and I'm ensconced in this little office, being attacked by flies, seriously wondering if I'll ever get this finished. If you end up holding this in your hand, reading these lines, you'll know that I can actually practise what I preach!

You yourselves have all shown us on many occasions how utterly determined you all can be, whether it be in schoolwork, sport or simply when you do your utmost to pester your mother and me to buy things for you! However, it is an inevitable fact of life that you will have setbacks. I have had people attempt to derail my teaching career on more than one occasion, but thankfully I am still rolling and enjoying the job. It's important to stick by your values, what you know to be right and press on. Set yourselves goals, be ambitious – as I was saying earlier – and nurture that stickability, which will ultimately make whatever you achieve that much more enjoyable.

E

is for

EDUCATION

"I pay the schoolmaster, but 'tis the schoolboys that educate my son."

Ralph Waldo Emerson (*Journals*)

EDUCATION

I love this quote. It was penned by an American philosopher no less and it is stronger for its stark simplicity. For me, it represents something often overlooked and is a big part of what each educational establishment that I ever attended actually left me with. I remember bits and pieces of what I was taught in the various subjects (and fortunately remember a little more than that from my A level subjects), but the vast majority of information I collated and stuffed into my head in my school (and university) years has long since gone. Happily, in its place I do have a real love of learning and crucially have the ability to learn, and that is something that will hopefully be lifelong. Fortunately, as well as this, I have picked up a variety of skills, including social interaction, the true meaning of friendship and, crucially, the importance of perspectives. They may be rather an odd group to single out, but these are skills that I have recourse to every day of my life and much of what I picked up at school determines how I respond in those situations, so this makes them particularly important.

Of course, all this starts in primary school, and these skills are honed over the years that follow. Your mother and I have done our best to give you the best education possible and we hope very much that you are gaining a lot from it and will continue to do throughout your lives. As I sit here now, I fondly remember all of you starting in your small village primary school, how we walked you to school holding your hands (your other hands clasping your blue satchels or your lunch boxes), teaching you how to cross the road day after day, before handing you over to your teachers for six hours before going back to collect you and coming home with all manner of things that you had made, drawn or written during the day. As you progressed through the years, we saw how you became more independent, more self-assured, but at the same time, a little more self-conscious. What has really pleased us is how you have all tried so hard to do your best, not only academically – and you really have tried there – but in other aspects of school life such as sport, debating and music. How proud we have been of everything you have achieved. You have learnt many skills and will, I'm sure, be left with the ability to continue your own learning journeys

Education

well beyond school – and in a multitude of ways. You have also been keenly aware of opportunities and taken them and done so in a way that I was never able to. You will never regret that and it will allow you to look back on your schooldays with real affection and a strong sense of achievement. I do, however, wish we could have afforded for you to have gone on more school trips, but we hope we have partly made up for that with some lovely family holidays over the years, which have left us with yet more lovely memories. They have also been a wonderful form of education – for all of us – as we have explored different countries together and tried to make the most of every day we had there. I hope that we will have plenty more of these and continue the learning experience together.

F

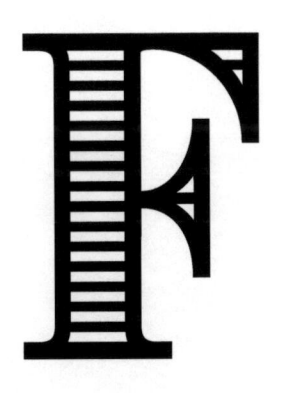

is for

FAMILY
(AND FRIENDS)

> *"Treasure your families — the future of humanity passes by way of the family."*
>
> John Paul II (Speech, 1982)

FAMILY (AND FRIENDS)

Gosh, this has to be the most important of all! For a younger person setting out on the journey of life, family may be something that you want to show that you can break away from, whilst deep down never wanting to lose that special, close, loving connection that family provides. Certainly, for young people, parents can be embarrassing, a bit overpowering, occasionally too keen to admonish and a relic of a distant age when everyone knew a lot less than they do today! I know from many a comment thrown in my direction that much of that is considered to be true in our household! However, we love being relics, we love being ridiculed and taken to task over our clothes and our attitudes – it's how we were just yesterday. We thought we were hip, but as soon as we had children, we lost all street cred and took on every guise of the square – we are now the joke. The wonderful thing is we love it, as it comes with being parents. We laugh, as we know it will be you one day. Just as we had to show our parents how to use the VHS player or the peculiar ins and outs of the remote control or Ceefax, you now come along and sort out our smartphones and our internet connectivity issues! So the world goes round.

Families are the bedrock of life and for me they have to come first – over work, social life, everything. It's what we do our daily grind for. My awesome parents certainly did and the same was true for your mother's equally awesome parents. Families are what you depend on when life smites you and when it rewards you. Families are there to share happy times and sad times. Indeed, it can be said that with a strong family behind you, you can cope with the worst of misfortunes. Families are also there to relish achievements and to enjoy special occasions. Families are there to share your hopes and fears. Families are there to love and cherish and to bring out the best in you and what you want to be. In short, families are special – extra special – and through my own experience as a child in a happy family and through having you all, I have no doubt that this is true.

The older we get, the more we realise how wonderful families are. Some of us are lucky enough to have lovely partners to share our lives with (I have certainly been blessed there) and we share the same journey for years and years, support and cherish each other, as well as being able to marvel joyfully together at how children develop. We obviously want the same for you and hope that you find those special people and can have your own families. When we are young, families are the protective shield that we can retreat behind as well as the home of all things loving and wonderful; when we are older, that is still true, but they are also a source of immense pride and fascination.

If we are further blessed, we have grandparents – and I *was* blessed. I learnt so much from my four grandparents and they certainly shaped my life and gave me perspectives that people I knew without grandparents never had. The memories of their wisdom, their sense of fun and their love remain very much with me today and I am a better person for that experience. My parents and grandparents certainly taught me the importance of family and family ties and I have never forgotten that. The same has been true of your mother. Even though she has lived here all her life, her parents and grandparents have instilled in her the values, skills and attitudes of her Italian heritage and much of that she has been able to share with you. That has added a lot of richness and colour to so much of our family life and instilled in you all a love of Italy and Italian culture, which is tremendous.

Now I mention my parents and grandparents and recall them saying so often how vital their siblings were to them, not only when they were younger when they could share many happy times together, but crucially when they were much older too. Fortunately, I am so blessed with a wonderful brother and sister and your mother with a wonderful brother, and I very much hope that you will feel the same about each other. You will, I promise, gain so much pleasure seeing how each other's household develops and you will continue to share many very special moments together many, many years into the future. Enjoy them!

Now families are great, but in this ever-expanding world they may not always be close by. There may be moments of tension, there may be differences in attitudes and ideas and although they are family, you didn't choose them! Friends, however, are different. In many ways, friends are as important as family. They share the ups and downs of life, they keep you balanced and give you attitudes and perspectives that families may not. They are certainly vital too. Happily, you have all got nice friends – as far as we are aware! – and you will make many more. Unfortunately, I have never been the best at keeping in touch with old friends, as my generation is pre-Facebook and pre-Instagram, but I still happily have some fantastic mates with whom I can get together and have a good time, even after a while apart. These are true friends. I have one whom I have known since we were at nursery school together – that's almost fifty years – and we still meet up, have a great time and share the good and bad that life throws at us. Yep, friends are special too. Make friends and keep as many as you can, especially the positive ones who really value your friendship – you'll never regret it.

G

is for

GRATITUDE

"A joy and pleasant thing it is to be thankful."

The Book of Common Prayer (*Psalm 147:1*)

GRATITUDE

We all like to be thanked for things – especially maybe for doing something where we have gone above and beyond what's expected – but in reality, we just like our efforts, however small, to be acknowledged, as it shows respect and it makes us feel good. Sadly, all too frequently, our efforts can be overlooked and our immense contributions can be undervalued, so it makes a really pleasant impression on us when someone actually takes the trouble to say thank you and I do hope all of you keep showing your gratitude as often as you can.

As adults, you see, so many people get out of the habit of thanking people, especially in a formal way, especially once they have passed through the negativity of adolescence and entered the whirlwind of daily working life. However, gratitude is such a positive, feel-good sentiment – you are giving, it costs nothing and both parties benefit. It's win-win! In her excellent book on positive psychology, Bridget Grenville-Cleave states that gratitude is one of the top five character strengths associated with life satisfaction (the others being zest, love, hope and curiosity – all of which I cover in this book). She suggests a few things that you should do to develop an 'attitude of gratitude':

- » Keep a gratitude journal – spend fifteen minutes a week writing down all the things from the last seven days that you feel grateful for.
- » Write a thank you card or letter, describing what somebody did and how it influenced you.
- » At the end of each day, think of three good things that went well for you.

I agree with all of these – although I have to say that I have only done a couple of them and both all too infrequently. However, as my grandmother advised, I do very frequently count my blessings, especially in trickier times. That's something that life certainly teaches you. Yes, you reach out and try for things and you see others doing the same. Sometimes, there is success and all is rosy, but there are inevitably times when you are frustrated by people, by life and feel let down, or when you make mistakes or do something out of character. When things are not going quite right, look around at what is, especially family and friends, and feel blessed. There is always something that you can feel grateful for, even if it was just having the good fortune to be conceived and to be given life! In effect, by showing or feeling gratitude, what you are doing is celebrating the positives in life and enabling them to dominate and repress the negatives. Again, what life has taught me is that when you associate with positive people (who often have spadeloads of gratitude!), you feel immeasurably better and it has all kinds of health and wellbeing benefits. You then become one and other positive people gravitate towards you. OK, in life and the workplace it can be jolly hard to avoid the negative, ungrateful elements, as they are everywhere, but do try to find time to seek out that other breed who will enrich your lives and to whom you will undoubtedly feel grateful.

.

H

is for

HOPE

"He that lives in hope danceth without music."

George Herbert (*Jacula Prudentum*, 1640)

HOPE

This is no less than a force within you that pushes you further because it's positive and imagining the best. Call it optimism if you will, but hope is the term I will use. A world without hope would be a desolate place, but why make it so? Yes, there is plenty to be depressed about if you want there to be, but why should you be when there are so many benefits to embracing hope. Apart from love, it is the best four-letter word there is – there are plenty of bad ones, so why not opt for a good one?!

You know, there have been multitudes of studies over the decades focusing on the benefits of hope, and you won't be surprised to learn that they include recovering more quickly from illnesses and living longer. Quite simply, it's a positive mindset that allows you to feel happier, less stressed and able to get more from life, and that is exactly where we, as parents, want you to be.

To my mind, there are various degrees of hope and I subscribe to ones where there is at least some possibility of that hope being realised. I no longer hope to be a top sportsman or to own a mansion – it's just not going to happen. However, I do hope that you like something about this book (!) and also that a few others might find it interesting too, but I am in no way expecting it to top the bestseller charts. What this small element of hope does is that it keeps me motivated, it keeps me writing and it keeps me thinking of you and your future, which is a lovely way of passing the time.

Back in the 1990s, the Prime Minister John Major introduced the National Lottery. This has turned out to be a jolly good idea as it has funded so many good causes and notably helped Great Britain's Olympic team finish second in the 2016 Olympics, which was an amazing achievement, not least because we even left China trailing in our wake. People still play a form of lottery week in, week out, as it offers them hope. They may not expect to win, but there is that small chance, that ray of an opportunity that they cling to. My grandparents were the same. They had a set of numbers based on family birthdays and played weekly and their joy came in imagining a big lottery win that they could divide up amongst the family members. Although the chances of winning were really negligible – and for the main draw, they are just that – they got a lot of pleasure from the miniscule speck of hope that it represented. For me, that hope would not be enough, and if I play the lottery in any form, I fully expect to lose and do it for the good causes, but I love the idea that for some people, it gives them a level of excitement that they cling to every week despite the near certainty of failure.

My biggest hope is that you will all live long, successful, happy and fulfilling lives, as will your children and grandchildren. That, for me, is a real hope with every chance of becoming reality, and for that I get a huge amount of pleasure every bit as overwhelming as my grandparents' love of the announcement of the weekly lottery numbers.

I

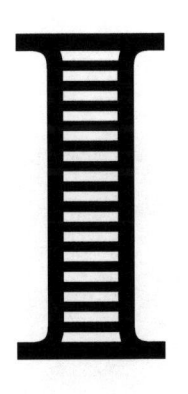

is for

INTERESTS

"All intellectual improvement arises from leisure"

James Boswell (*Life of Samuel Johnson,* 1791)

INTERESTS

I have a good friend who has really mastered the art of the work/life balance. I have to envy him, as he has always found time to pursue his hobbies and interests, and not at the expense of family life either. He is remarkably happy and positive as a result. He supports a football team that frequently wins – that's Manchester United, whereas I struggle these days with Arsenal – he collects things, he exercises well and enjoys music and keeping in close touch with friends. Fantastic! I must have chosen the wrong profession, as I am always pressed for time and constantly berate myself for not spending as much quality time with you all as I would like. I know I need to relax more and pursue more interests – for me it's mañana, mañana. For you it need not be. You all know the benefits of exercise and do plenty of it and the challenge will be to keep this going. However, you are definitely setting yourselves up for a better life by being more disciplined there. You all like playing a musical instrument, maybe not to virtuoso level as yet, but you can all play something for pleasure and amusement and that's wonderful – again, I have dabbled, but have never had the time to pursue as much as I would have liked. Again, mañana, mañana. How far away is retirement?!

Funnily enough, as you get older, interests seem to gain in importance. Now I don't know if it's because we subconsciously plan for said retirement or simply become more chilled. If so, I have still got some chilling to go. When I think about it, I do consciously make time to have a relaxing moment or two, usually at weekends. You know I love the newspaper and the cappuccino thing, as well as a bit of golf or jogging, but for me these aren't real 'interests', important though they are. What you need are interests that fulfil you in some way, that maybe also enhance you, take you out of your comfort zone and make you feel happy with yourself and what you are achieving. That could be from as wide a range as learning another language to collecting things. Funnily enough, I think that families need to have joint interests too. These are great, as they provide such a wealth of memories and experiences. We have had such fun travelling together, watching films, playing board games and even cycling. Admittedly these are more of a holiday occurrence for frazzled teachers, but they are still interests of a sort and wonderful for being so, as they do offer a certain type of enjoyment and fulfilment for us as a family. Don't forget that interests help to dispel worries and negativity and they add variety to your life. They also provide you with the opportunity to press the reset button, which in turn may well help you to unclutter your mind and make key decisions in a more balanced way.

Now, you have a great advantage over us old 'uns and you have the strength, stamina and, crucially, time, to make good your existing interests and crucially to take up new ones. Maybe I'm being a bit old-fashioned here, but it seems to be that it's good to have interests in quite different areas. I believe it's good to have a sport that you play, an instrument that you play and a more cerebral interest of some sort, such as reading or puzzles. Why? Because having interests is such an enormous contributor to a sense of wellbeing, of achieving that sense of completeness in life that we all crave. If you start young, you can achieve so much. Saying that, you are never too old to start! Here I am now writing this for you. I recently had piano lessons for a number of years – I enjoyed them and surprised myself with how much I could manage to learn. I still want to learn the steel drums, as I associate them so much with my father and his own interests. Although he's been gone for so many years now, it still gives me that possibility of a new connection with him. That's my plan, anyway!

Whatever interests you choose to pursue, enjoy them and give them as much time as you can. They will enrich you, keep you positive and provide you with a real sense of achievement throughout your life. Aim to outdo your dad in this area – but saying that, it won't be too hard!

J

is for

JOY

"Joy, beautiful radiance of the gods."

Friedrich von Schiller (*An die Freude,* 1785)

JOY

This is a lovely one! Remember when, as little ones, you could scarcely get to sleep the night before a birthday or on Christmas Eve, so excited were you by the prospect of what you might find wrapped up for you the next day. You were anticipating the joy you would feel owning new toys, sweets, clothes and books, and so many would also be a complete surprise, which made it all extra special. Even now, you do not want either myself or your mother to know what you are wrapping before we open it. You so kindly want us to experience a bit of joy – just as we did (and still do) – and you try so hard to achieve it. We're the olds, your parents, and you're doing it for us. It's really touching.

I have to say, one of the best things about being a parent is that you can bring joy to your children. As parents, we want to do it as often as possible, but, as we have found, as you get older, money = joy is a really accurate equation, so we are frequently bordering on skint to keep you adolescents in something vaguely akin to joy before truculence returns. That fleeting joy at the sight of the twenty-pound note nestling in your hands is still lovely to behold – only slightly offset by a slight pang of anxiety at the lighter wallet that it emerged from.

What you need to do is keep searching for that joyful experience. It may indeed emanate from money. I used to work with accountants who were obsessed with the stuff and talking about it, earning it and spending it was what gave so many of them such joy that it offset the mind-numbing tedium of much of their work. I couldn't operate like that, so I attempted to find some joy in teaching children languages. And yes, I have found it in teaching – certainly not all the time, but on quite a few occasions. I love seeing my students succeed and prosper. I get a real kick when I can give them good marks, good reports and most of all, when they achieve beyond expectations in their exams. I can well recall how I felt when I ran chess, public speaking and debating teams, and when we won matches and made our way through round after round of competitions. I can recall the same when sports teams of mine have won. The joy is there because you experience a real sense of achievement after such a lot of hard work. When it all pays off, there is clear joy and it's a great feeling.

Joy

So what is joy, then? Is it just happiness in a different guise? No, it's a real moment of exhilaration, and such moments stay in the memory and you can hark back to them in bad times to convince yourself that life is not really so bad. Now, you guys have brought us so much joy and keep doing so well into your teens, and I'm sure you always will. I can define periods of my life by the joy that you have all brought me and I know that your mother would say the same. I can recall the elation I felt when you came into the world, all happy and healthy; I can recall first steps, first few words, first time you saw rain, first birthday parties (and subsequent ones), you giggling with friends, scoring in sports matches, getting good reports, reading together, cuddling together, laughing together. The truth is that with you all the joy thankfully never ends. I hear the conversations that you have and marvel at how well you speak; look at you and feel pride and how you look, dress and conduct yourselves; and am always delighted when we take the mickey out of each other and I see your smiles and hear your laughter. What more could any parent want?

K

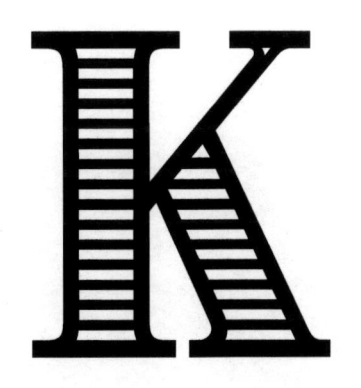

is for

KINDNESS

> *"So many gods, so many creeds*
> *So many paths that wind and wind,*
> *While just the art of being kind*
> *Is all the sad world needs."*

Ella Wheeler Wilcox (*The World's Need,* 1917)

KINDNESS

These words of the American author Ella Wheeler Wilcox are, indeed, so true. Despite the horror stories we hear on the news all too regularly, I would argue that the world has far more kind people in it than otherwise – if only we saw and heard of more stories of kind deeds, we might be a little less worried about the state of the world in the twenty-first century.

Happily, in our own lives, we come across many kind individuals and remember their acts and gestures and, in case you think such people are lacking in your lives, you meet more of them the older you get – or bizarrely that is how has seemed to me. I can well recall that when I was very small, say two or three years old, I did not meet a kind soul of my age at all – not one! Yes, my family were lovely and balanced my view of human nature, but the children around me were, frankly, horrific and this is something I remember to this day. So when I met my friend Matt when I was four years old and discovered someone my one age with such a nice, kind and fun-loving personality, I could hardly believe it; we became firm friends immediately and still are today, almost fifty years later! In my school days, my impression was that my peers became kinder people as they progressed through their teens and my own circle of friends grew as a result. In teaching, you see how students progress from being very pleasant, enthusiastic young things at age eleven, then are forced to combat adolescence and all its effects on personality (many still cope very admirably with this) and then become more relaxed and easier to work with in their sixth form years. It will always be thus.

However, even in those challenging teenage years, they still show many acts of great kindness and as teachers we are in a privileged position to be able to praise and encourage these. Obviously as parents, your mother and I try to do the same with you and you all respond very well to it. That said, there is an important distinction to point out here – emptying the dishwasher is not an example of kindness; it's a chore, a household chore to help the world go round! The same is true for bringing your towels and clothes downstairs or folding the washing. However, making your mother a cup of tea is an act of kindness and you certainly do plenty of that – where's the whisky for your old man, then?

As I said earlier, it is certainly true that kind acts and gestures really make such a difference and they affect how people view you and their memory of you. Equally, acts of kindness may well bring you benefits later if you are lucky – though that's not why you should be doing them! My aunt and grandad paid for my driving lessons – which were not an inconsiderable sum at the time – and I have been forever grateful. In doing so, though, they had enabled me to not only have my independence and to acquire an important life skill, but to be able to drive up to visit them in the north-east. I would still have liked to have done this more often to reward their kindness more fully, but was still able to do it occasionally and I will never forget the impact that their real act of kindness had on my life. Very soon after, I was posted as an English assistant to a school in a very small French town near the Belgian border and it was a desperately sad and lonely place with little going on. Happily, I was able to buy a car, make and visit new friends further away and visit the 'happening' towns in West Belgium. That made a real difference to my enjoyment of that year and helped improve my French – a subject that I now teach for a living.

L

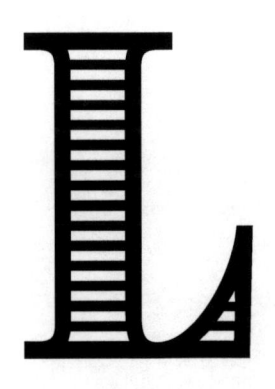

is for

LOVE

"There is only one happiness in life, to love and be loved"

George Sand (*Letter to Lina Calamatta*, 1862)

LOVE

This is what this book is all about. I have to start with an extract from my favourite passage from the Bible, which is the classic one from 1 Corinthians 13:

"Love is patient and kind; it is not jealous or conceited or proud; love is not ill-mannered or selfish or irritable; love does not keep a record of wrongs; love is not happy with evil, but is happy with the truth. Love never gives up; and its faith, hope and patience never fail."

This was so beautifully read by a colleague at our own wedding and I attempted to do it justice at my sister's wedding some years later – and I felt privileged to do so. Love starts when you meet someone and get married, then it joyfully spreads to the creation of a new generation, from where it spreads further and further and gets stronger and stronger. There are so many things that I'd like to say to you all and there are never the opportunities to say them quite as I would like and that is why you are reading this now. This entry is just such an example. Luckily, I really know what I'm talking about with this one! I was born lucky in that I was born into a loving family and so was your mother. My, it makes such a difference to the way that you cope with life. Yes, I was lucky, and so were you!

When you were all born, it was love at first sight – it was even love before then when you were kicking and moving around in the womb and when we saw you on those scan photographs. The anticipation built up and you all arrived perfectly and we were so relieved. When we held you all in our arms when you were babies, smiled and chatted to you and covered you with kisses, we were the happiest people in the world. We knew we had won the lottery and will always be so grateful that we had you. That love that we felt then, we feel just as much now and we cannot help but let you know. Yes, parents can be annoying and they can be uncool, but we will always be there for you and will love you no matter what.

We really hope that you will experience the joy of your own children one day and we know that you will so willingly show that unconditional love for them that we will always feel for you. Having children is a magical experience – an unbelievable one in so many ways – and we love seeing how you are developing into such fine adults. We love hearing your voices, your chatter, your laughter, your singing, even your bickering (!) and put-downs. It's all so special to us and it means everything as you with your lives have opened new chapters for us and your family, opportunities for us to feel such love and pride as we have never felt before.

Now we won't be here forever and we will only share those chapters with you for a while, but they will I'm sure continue to be happy ones and we hope that you will have such wonderful times of your own to share with your own families in the future. Remember though that even when we are no longer here, we will still be with you – our love will always be there. We will always be watching over you and we will always be with you. We will love you always – I promise.

M

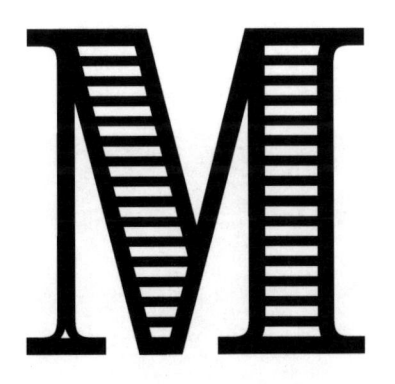

is for

MONEY

"And money is like muck, not good except it be spread."

Francis Bacon (*Of Seditions and Troubles*, 1625)

MONEY

Quotes on money abound! Although I like the above, my favourite is from Ecclesiastes ch. 10 v. 19 "Wine maketh merry : but money answereth all things". It's a great biblical quote and one that a good friend of mine who came into a large sum of money early in adulthood would certainly agree with. He was at a difficult point in his life when the job he had long sought had not materialised and his career prospects looked less and less rosy. His father was dying and he was having problems with social services and, indeed, with his own health. As if he hadn't suffered enough, he then had a car accident. By his own admission, he was so down that he was seriously considering ending it all. Then, like a 'deus ex machina', an aunt of his passed away and her will revealed that she had acquired a hidden skill of making money on the stock market, which ultimately led to him receiving a huge, life-changing sum of money. He then had a new much more positive outlook on life, which has not evaporated – indeed, he has bought property and used his money well. Having money certainly brought him happiness. Whilst money is not everything, having a good measure of it certainly oils the cogs of life and makes more things possible, so it is important, very important.

Now, I am not a money nut. When I worked in accountancy, I was surrounded by people who properly worshipped money. It consumed them and everyone around them and I hated it. I have since much preferred the more serene environment of the school staff room, where people certainly want as much money as they can get, but are not obsessed by it. Why, then, would they be in teaching? There are other important aspects to one's working life, such as making a positive difference to the lives of others. I decided at quite a young age that I would not allow my life to be dominated by money and the constant pursuit of it. My parents had been happy, and my grandparents – who had appreciably less – had been the same. For them, family, friends and interests had been their wealth and they made the most of all of them. People can so easily pursue money to the exclusion of all else, and that can make life far more stressful and less rewarding. What is the point of spending most of your lives away from your home and your families, working yourself to the ground in some far-flung part of the world and being, to all intents and purposes, an absent parent? I have had opportunities (and good ones) to work abroad in China and other countries and although such possibilities have had their attractions, such jobs are not for me. If it would have benefitted you and your mother to have once again been uprooted, then that may have been different, but we loved it so much here in the Cotswolds and you were so settled in your schools and friendship groups. I therefore did not have even the slightest inclination to change anything there – and rightly so.

You mustn't forget, though, that money is almost always hard earnt, and you mustn't be frivolous with it. Don't fritter it away. I never had much of it as a kid and when I was a student, that remained the same – I was living pretty hand to mouth at times, but it was a useful experience and I find it hard to spend much even now. If I feel I am being ripped off by anything or if a shop is selling something that appeals to me for anything like too much money, I am not interested. In fact, I am almost offended – how dare they be so greedy and treat people as mugs! Well, they do it because some mug will always buy the product at their asking price. My grandparents regularly used to say that you get what you pay for and there are no such things as bargains – hmm, not sure if I really agree. There are great bargains to be had in January sales and in flights and holiday destinations, for instance. Also, you can often find that food and prices for home furnishings can vary enormously in price, as can quotes for services. Every year, I look at our insurances and change some. It is important to be aware, though, that the cheapest of things are not always the best, the longest lasting, the most reliable. I can talk to you about poor insurance providers, poor televisions and dishwashers. No, do your research and look for good value – that's what it's all about. Will it do the job and not cause you issues down the line? You are already learning this – all of you – and you will be faced with making decisions about purchases throughout your lives and will need to stay on the ball.

The bottom line to all this is, quite simply, to respect money. I went through a period of my life when I made what I now consider to be rash moves with my career. They were exciting at first, but then became worrying. I am talking here about when I started my own businesses. They progressed certainly, but initially nowhere near as quickly as I hoped they would and I felt myself hurtling towards a cliff. Thank God I got myself further employment and disaster was averted. Again, I am not sure that I had planned things as well as I could have done. Don't be that cavalier, please. Learn from the old man! I am certainly pleased that you are all keen to work and have part-time jobs and that in doing so, you are learning about money and how it's usually only through hard graft that you come by it. You will certainly gain a lot through doing so.

Having said all that I have said above, I will certainly not be advising you as to how best to make lots of money. I am no expert in that direction. The important point is that the more educated, the more qualified and the more experienced you get, the easier it will be for you to land a good job, which will allow you to live comfortably and that's the least that we would want for you. You will find your own paths to money, but once you make it, please treat it well, as it can bite back nastily if it's disrespected!

N

is for

NATURE

> *"All my life through, the new sights of Nature made me rejoice like a child."*

Marie Curie (*Pierre Curie*)

NATURE

I love nature and, as you know, I'm glued to the television when nature programmes come on. There is no doubt that one of the great benefits of living in the Cotswolds is our proximity to some of the most beautiful scenery in Britain. However, even before we lived here, we would take off whenever we could to areas of the country where we could be close to nature, such as the Peak District, the north-east or Wales, where we could take out our walking boots and amble along, taking in the fresh air and marvel at the breath-taking views. It is so good for your health and wellbeing to get away from the hustle and bustle and unwind in the middle of somewhere different, somewhere where you feel at one with nature.

Now I have never been one for freshwater fishing (but that may change, who knows?) and I am quite taken by the idea of hiring a boat and drifting off along a lake or loch and casting a line for a few hours – more than anything just to experience the tranquillity of being in that setting, being able to admire the landscapes and being at one with nature. As you get older, you somehow relish those peaceful moments more and more and maybe getting close to nature becomes more important. I certainly take more notice of flowers, trees and birds nowadays and have learnt the names of many of them. I still compare poorly with my grandad (your great-grandfather on my father's side) who knew the names of so many of the plants and wildflowers, having learnt them as a boy. He would walk along and happily pick mushrooms and berries, eating them as he went, confident in his knowledge of what was safe and not. Whilst I would not recommend you do the same (!), it does suggest that when he was young, children were more in tune with nature than in subsequent generations and loved and respected it. He used to thoroughly enjoy walking his dogs along picturesque country lanes and holidaying in remote parts of Scotland where he felt at home with the beauty and peace that they offered. It kept him calm and happy, and he lived on well into his nineties.

I would urge you all to find time in your lives – busy as they will undoubtedly be – to explore the countryside, not just in Britain, of course, but to do so with an aim of learning more about it and appreciating how wonderful this world is in which we live. There will be many attempts in your lives to concrete over more and more of the countryside to build homes and businesses. It was ever thus, but in your generation and those to follow, I fear that there will be less and less to enjoy as more and more species suffer from this urban expansion. I hope very much that despite this, you will all find opportunities to get out there and enjoy the fresh air, maybe even taking up new hobbies (and I don't just mean fishing) which will allow you look forward to those breaks and encourage you to stay healthy and feel thankful for the beauty and wonder of the world around us.

O

is for

ORIGINALITY

> *"Insist upon yourself.
> Be original."*
>
> Ralph Waldo Emerson

ORIGINALITY

When I was school, I can remember friends saying to me that it was always a good thing to 'be original'. They were not specifying areas where it might have been of particular benefit, but were simply saying that it's cool to cultivate a different perspective whenever you can and it might well reap dividends. Yes, it can be a good thing to be a bit different from the norm and to surprise people. I can remember putting this to good effect when I was preparing for Oxbridge entrance and chose to read a significant number of Molière plays. Hardly earth-shatteringly original, but for someone of that age, it was rare and caught the eye. In later years, when applying for jobs, I have sometimes looked to incorporate a semblance of originality into my preparation, be it in the form of a report or presentation I have compiled or maybe in terms of facts, statistics or connections of various sorts that I have brought into the interview. It may not always work, but it will get you noticed.

In my professional life, in teaching or in business, I have always been keen to bring in new ideas and to alter perspectives, to look at being more creative in attempts to solve problems and move things forward. That can sometimes be welcomed and sometimes not. If you are the boss and you show an original approach, whether good or bad, you are frequently lauded, less so if you are lower down the scale and you may well not be taken seriously at all. Sadly, even though in life we claim to value originality, individuality and self-expression, many people are happy just to accept the status quo and to go with the flow and this has led to a real lack of originality that has hampered the progress of businesses. We have seen that recently with the financial difficulties of certain retail outlets. They have not sought this kind of approach, unlike their competitors, and have been left behind. It is the same with individuals. It is often the case that those with the courage to show originality reach the top and continue as successes when they get there. These people, because of their own penchant for the unexpected move, may sense this trait in others and help bring it out to their mutual benefit. Richard Branson springs to mind; having taken the plunge and opened a recording studio to help showcase the music of lesser-known artists, he chanced upon *Tubular Bells* by Mike Oldfield, saw its potential, released it to great acclaim and the rest is happy history.

In life and in business, you have opportunities to either work within the mould or to break it. You have but one precious life and can play the game as determined or you can choose to play your hand differently – when appropriate. It's worth considering the latter and you may be amazed where it gets you. An original approach to certain aspects of life requires a little courage, certainly, but it can be enjoyable and highly rewarding. It may take time to get an original idea heard and taken seriously and it will take great patience to see it through to a conclusion. You may be the only person initially to believe in an idea or an approach, but the more that you are able to expand the realms of possibilities both in your personal lives and in your professional ones, the more respect and admiration you will gain and the more successful you will be.

P
is for
PREPARATION

"Be prepared."

Robert Baden Powell (*Scouting for Boys*, 1908)

PREPARATION

'Be prepared' is the motto of the Scout Association, and what a good one it is too. It is not simply meant for those learning knots or for putting up tents, but for all aspects of life that may be faced in the future. When you have the opportunity to prepare well, so many of the tougher tasks in life become more manageable and even, dare I say it, enjoyable and personally satisfying. Public speaking immediately comes to mind. Even greats like Churchill had to put in preparation time, as he famously did in front of a mirror, no doubt cultivating that rousing oratorical style for which he became so famous. I have given many a speech myself and whilst I cannot pretend that I enjoy the experience, I make sure I prepare as thoroughly as I can and practise.

Saying that, I have always found wedding speeches a lot of fun – usually because you have an expectant and supportive audience, keen to enjoy any titbits of gossip or humour and often steadily becoming less inhibited through alcohol – and you are totally in control and foolishly allowed free rein for a few minutes. Speeches in a professional context are often far more nerve-wracking, as you are more likely to be judged on your performance – however, once again, you will have the best chance with a decent amount of prep.

Exams are an interesting one. You all know about these – all teenagers do, as they unfortunately have to face some potentially life-changing ones whilst still at school. Often these exams demand much more from you than those of your degree – they may not be as intellectually demanding as at that level, but there is certainly an art to preparing for and succeeding in public examinations taken at school. That generally means having an almost military approach to revision, which is pretty demanding for sixteen- and eighteen-year-olds! Preparation of some description has to be involved at whatever level you are operating. Yes, you have to work on learning the information, mastering the presentation style and doing past papers, but you must not forget the vital part played in getting plenty of sleep, doing a bit of exercise and eating properly. I know to my cost what happens if you skimp on those when under exam pressure – don't be the same. Start your exam preparation early and you will be much more in control and able to look after yourself which will in turn help you to do your best without so much stress. I know this is easier said than done and there is much to be said for taking the dissertation route whenever you can, but there will inevitably be times in life – maybe long after university, maybe in your professional life or in your quest to be life-long learners – for whatever reason, you might find yourselves once again faced with one of these dreaded tests and have to sit down at a desk with an exam paper and a ridiculously fast-moving clock! I still reckon I've yet to face my last exam. I'm in my fifties – can't think what it will be, but I'll be a lot more chilled about it than when I was in my teens and twenties, that's for sure. Life teaches you a lot!

Life has also taught me the value of preparing for all sorts of things when many people would simply be content to wing it. There are many examples but one of the best ones I can give you is when you meet people at a party. So many of my friends had (as young people) and still have (!) a set patter which they trot out to whomever they meet. They get people onto their favourite subject, be it travelling, cooking vegetarian dishes, eighties pop songs or the stock market and they are away. Having prepared their patter, they can stand there with constantly refilled glasses of prosecco, holding court all night, knowing when to slip in the amazing facts, the side-splitting gags, the mind-blowing incidents, you name it. Having rehearsed it hundreds of times, they are the life and soul – it also allows friends who have heard the same lines on multiple occasions the perfect opportunity to take the mickey, which only adds to the level of mirth and enjoyment of the occasion. I'm still working on mine but keep forgetting the lines as I go to so few parties these days!

In so many different ways, preparation can give you the edge. I'd say it's vital when you are going to need something from somebody or when you are likely to be faced with a difficult conversation with somebody or, of course, the job interview. Rehearse the conversations in your mind, imagine the worst situation or question and think how you will respond. Make sure you look your best, think about body language and what you absolutely must mention before it's all over. Just a bit of thought beforehand will make a positive outcome that much more likely.

Even in something as humdrum as a car journey, I'd again throw in the motto, as there is much that can go wrong with a motor! As you know, whenever we have a longish journey ahead, I always do the checks on the car as I have to do my best to make sure we get there. Cars can be temperamental as well as dangerous so it is always preparation time well spent – indeed, I'd say it was vital as regular checks on the roadworthiness of vehicles always are. I will add that you should always be prepared to change your car if you have doubts about it or lose confidence in it for some reason. It is never worth taking a risk with a car, even when it comes to the driver – it must be right. If you're not happy, don't get in. You are all too precious to take unnecessary risks there – remember that!

If you accept that you will need to 'be prepared' for the big moments, the exams, the conversations, the interviews etc., you will also be more inclined to prepare yourself mentally for other events in your lives, positive or otherwise and it will help you cope better and lead to a much more successful outcome. Good luck!

Q

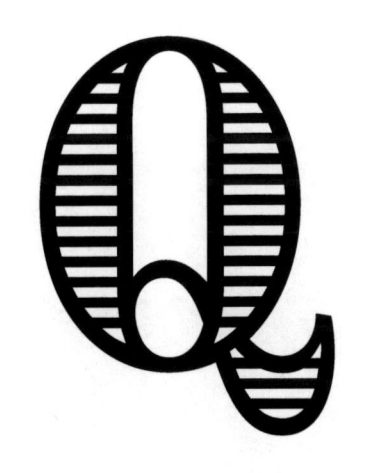

is for

QUESTIONING

"The important thing is not to stop questioning. Curiosity has its own reason for existing."

Albert Einstein

QUESTIONING

In life it is so easy to believe everything you read or hear and to blindly follow a particular orthodoxy or creed, because that is how it's always been. In these days of crackpot rulers and fake news, there is an increasing need to be more discerning and to question what information you are fed. The internet is awash with all kinds of trashy news and advertising and it is important to develop a mindset where you question what you see and hear.

Personal data is a key area these days. It is so easy to be fooled by people pretending to be police, bank officials or lawyers who insist that they need your passwords to be able to stop attempts by thieves to steal your money. It is a simple fact that you never need to hand over such details and should there be an issue with your money, it is far safer to drop into your branch and get it sorted that way. There are so many scams out there and so many crooks who are able to use ever more devious means to get hold of your hard-earned cash, but don't let them! Adopt a questioning mentality and put them on the spot – it's amazing how quickly the phone call will end or you may encounter anger and irritation, a sure sign that something is not right.

I had a splendid conversation with a local policeman a couple of years back; he spoke of his own questioning mentality and how that was so useful in his job, enabling him to be alert to things that looked abnormal or suspicious in some way when he was doing his sweep of the area in his car. He was urging me to do the same and to be attentive to anything odd that might suggest suspicious activity and to report it. I have to say that when I have reported something like this, I'm not sure it has been taken that seriously and I distinctly remember difficulties I have had getting positive responses on occasions – such as when I saw a horse bolting down the A45 – but it won't stop me trying if I think it is merited. I can well remember being burgled many years ago and just a few days prior to this, I saw a couple sitting in their car for a long while outside our house. That was not so uncommon in that particular area of London and although it did not seem right, I regret doing nothing. My suspicions were aroused, but for whatever reason I did nothing about it and the house was ransacked soon after. I didn't even have the car's registration number to give to the police. You live and learn! When I next saw a suspicious vehicle outside my house some years later, I certainly did approach it and the two gentleman inside soon took off – it turned out, however, they were two undercover detectives doing a stake-out of a neighbouring property and their activity later led to a number of arrests in our road.

I must say that as I have got older, experienced more of the world, watched more documentaries and taken on board plenty of Martin Lewis's advice, I find myself far more inclined to be suspicious and question the necessity of certain things. I have much enjoyed making a fuss about having to show my boarding card in non-duty free shops at airports, taking insurance companies to task over hidden petty costs or why it takes the council so long to repair potentially life-threatening potholes.

Finally, ask questions of yourselves all the time. Why am I doing certain things? Where am I heading? How am I presenting myself? Am I making the most of my talents and my time? Am I neglecting things? Am I neglecting people? Always give yourselves time to reflect and question your inner self – and do so pretty harshly. It will keep you sharp and protect you from having regrets as you let life pass by.

R

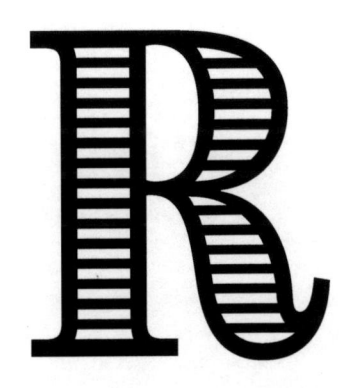

is for

REFLECTION

"I love the man that can smile in trouble, that can gather strength from distress, and grow brave by reflection."

Thomas Paine

REFLECTION

Now, I do this a lot, maybe too much. Why? Because life is special and, as I was hinting in the previous chapter, it is so easy to let it go by in the daily whirlwind without fully taking in the wonder of it in all its forms and equally, it is important to learn lessons from life's experiences.

I think back, for instance, to joyful times when you were all small and to times when your mother and I went off on holidays before you were born. All kinds of events come to mind – weddings, christenings, confirmations, parties, family gatherings. I also try hard to keep hold of other, more fleeting, moments, not necessarily when notable things happened, but things which captured a mood, an emotion, a turning point. I very frequently remember relatives and friends who have passed on and always consider how proud they would be of what you have achieved and how wonderfully you are growing up. Family was so important to them and a big part of what they talked about and reminisced about themselves.

Obviously I reflect on my career, on the jobs that I have had and where I am now, but often with a different aim in mind: I think about what I have learnt and that helps me be more in control of what I do in the future. When times are good, I enjoy the moment, but if dark clouds appear, I always think back to what I have achieved and that realigns my perspectives, which helps.

One thing I have hardly ever done is keep a diary – quite simply because after a day at work and an evening's preparation, I'm always too tired to put pen to paper again. I often wish that I had done so of course, particularly when I try and remember when something happened or how I was feeling at a particular moment in time. Maybe I could have simply written one-word entries, such as 'shattered', 'overworked', 'stressed'. The splendid Welsh actor Richard Burton, whom I very much admire, did himself keep a diary and quite a thick tome it turns out to be too. So much happened in his everyday life – interesting people, fascinating places, glamour, glitz, parties, money – but in spite of all of that, there were days that he could only sum up in the one word – 'booze'. I hope that seven more years of teaching won't lead me to do the same!

Well, anyway, I have little written to fall back on, yet I do have a really good memory of certain parts of my life, particularly my younger years, my headship years, my earlier years with your mother, your early years and that's great. I remember them as I have reflected on them a lot and they have become firmly engrained in my memory, even many conversations word for word. I think a diary is a really good idea, by the way. If you have the time, go for it, but make sure you take the trouble to read your entries back at some stage. They might be an emotional rollercoaster when you do, but why not? What's the motivation to continue if you feel that your words won't be re-read by your slightly older and wiser self at some point in the not-too-distant future? If that isn't possible, before you turn in at night, think of a few good things that happened to you during the course of the day and take those thoughts to bed with you. Although it may be hard, dispense with the less positive thoughts, as these run amok late at night and can often be dealt with much more effectively after a decent night's sleep anyway.

However you choose to do it, either by sitting comfortably sipping a cappuccino, a nice glass of claret or flicking through some old photos whilst listening to some of your favourite tracks, take yourselves back regularly to times you shared with us as kids, times you had with the rest of your family, your friends. I'm not ashamed to say that I do it frequently and I keep to the good memories – and there are many – and they always cheer me up, sort out my perspectives on life and remind me that I really have been blessed.

S

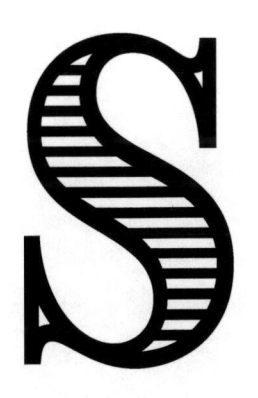

is for

SENSITIVITY

> *"I shook the habit off*
> *Entirely and for ever, and again*
> *In Nature's presence stood, as now I stand,*
> *A sensitive being, a creative soul."*

William Wordsworth (*The Prelude*, 1850)

SENSITIVITY

You know I'm more sensitive than you think – now there's a shocker! "Aha!" I hear you say. "You would say that, as it suits the demands of this chapter!" But no, sensitivity is something that has helped me through many happy and more challenging moments in my life, and before you complain that I don't show enough sensitivity to the cat, so I must be wrong, let me assure you that when I refer to her as a 'flea-bitten old ratbag', I do so with the greatest affection – I'm sure she knows that I'm only joking!

Now I'm sure we all know plenty of people whose

only sensitivity is to the weight of their wallet and who would be only too happy to sell their grandmother if it would give them a leg-up to a more luxurious and high-profile existence. I genuinely feel sorry for these people as they have lost something very precious in life – the capacity for real affection and care for others. I know it's much harder as you progress up the career ladder and take on ever-greater responsibility for more and more people, but an understanding and love for others on a human level need not be a casualty. There used to be a wonderful American television series a few years ago in which bosses of large, successful companies would spare a week in their busy schedules to go and work undercover as a low-status employee in their own company. They had to appreciate how tough certain jobs were and how some of their employees worked so hard yet found it difficult to provide adequately for their families and this opened their eyes. What was so heart-warming, though, was how these same bosses would then so happily reward those they had worked alongside during that week with promotions, gifts of money, holidays and anything that would make the lives of these employees that much easier and rewarding. Such bosses are great – they are at the top of the pile but have not lost their basic humanity. Most people would walk through walls for such people. If you ever reach such giddy heights of success yourselves, please make sure you look after those below you. I certainly aimed to do just that in all my management roles – and I know that I achieved it. When I was a head, I can well recall inspectors admitting to me that when grilling my staff in interviews, they had tried to elicit criticism of me and failed to do so. All my colleagues were apparently full of praise. I could hardly believe it at the time and when I left the job, quite a few staff asked if they might work for me again at some point in the future. Such comments were lovely and I'll never forget them; they were, I assume, the result of all the improvements I made both to the school and to their working conditions. I was sensitive to their needs and respected them – rightly so, as they were my greatest resource. It made me wish I'd stayed longer!

My sensitivity (and that's how I'll put it!) has also protected me on many occasions. It has helped me co-exist with some challenging people, be they students and colleagues – knowing what to say and do and not and as a result avoiding many a painful confrontation. I have always been careful when writing to people, when writing school reports, when embarking on tricky and sensitive conversations. People can react in some strange ways at times and it's always best to show them respect and sensitivity – at least at the outset, unless their behaviour becomes unreasonable. That said, the protective aspect in your sensitive nature allows you to prepare yourself well for certain situations – the once bitten, twice shy syndrome – as it is natural to want to shield yourself from unpleasantness and harm.

So my message here is to always respect the gentler, more sensitive side to your nature, your emotional, caring side and please keep nurturing it and never lose it. The more sensitivity you have to others and to your own needs, the better you will be as a human being and the happier you will feel when you look back on what you have achieved in life. You certainly cannot be all things to all people and we all have regrets, but hopefully these will be minor in comparison to all the good that you will do.

T

is for

TIME

> *"I wasted time, and now doth time waste me."*

William Shakespeare (*Richard II*, 1597)

TIME

I remember hearing a colleague many years ago delivering a school assembly on the subject of time. It was quite powerful stuff! The teacher began his address by quoting from his first history lesson with a new teacher at his own school. That teacher's first act was to point up at the clock on his wall and exclaim that time was their greatest enemy as it would always march on and would take no prisoners. Time was uncompromising and dangerous and they would do well to respect it. You know, he was right. When you are young, you care little for time, really. You have the energy to want to fill it with as much as you can, which is tremendous, but young people rarely have the perspective to respect time in the way that they should and do the things that matter for their future in the slots that have appeared for them. Social media, social life, television and lie-ins all grab more than their fair share, and it's boring to plan your time anyway, isn't it? It's hard to be disciplined in that respect, I know, and I'm pleased to say that you guys generally buck the trend, but it doesn't get easier, I warn you! In a sense, boring though it may be, do keep an eye on where you want to be by when. In the first chapter, I mentioned the need for a career plan of some sort and with that I'd add some sort of a vague life plan too. Why? Because as you grow older, time moves faster! Time is plentiful when you are young and then when you reach your fifties, it seems that it is beginning to run away with you and you can't slow it down!

I remember reading a parish letter from our old vicar and he talked about this very thing in his message to us. He talked about being proud to be ten, excited to be twenty, happy to be thirty, concerned to be forty, alarmed at being fifty and resigned on reaching sixty. This might suggest that his thirties were his best decade and yes, they are great years often blessed with young children and career progression. I'd say that your forties are pretty good too, as long as you stay healthy. Normally you can work hard in those decades and have the energy to achieve lots of things and because you are still young career-wise, you are very employable right through. At fifty though, that begins to change. Saga appears, doctors want to give you regular health checks, you suddenly become a bit less employable and you have to start respecting your body more. You also think that because you have reached this milestone, you should have this or that or should have achieved this or that – and *haven't*! So be prepared. Saying all that, I don't feel any different to when I was in my forties, so I still have ambitions and plans to do things. How I'll feel at sixty I do not know, but I do hope I will be fully retired and planning where to travel to and enjoying each day as it comes, doing lots of things that time does not allow me to do now.

U

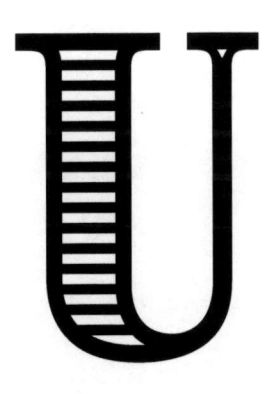

is for

UNDERSTANDING

> *"I shall light a candle of understanding in thine heart, which shall not be put out."*

Apocrypha (II Esdras, ch14 v25)

UNDERSTANDING

Being understanding is not something that comes easily to everyone, but it really helps the world go round. People make mistakes, do things inadvertently that cause offence, have things happen to them that necessitate changes to plans and put people out and there are many other such instances that would benefit from a measure of understanding from the other party. The trouble is that many refuse to see beyond the simple fact that something has not been done and in today's frenetic world when money and time are such vital commodities, anything that upsets the balance and causes a slowdown is serious business. Imagine you are delivering some merchandise and have been delayed by traffic or illness and you know full well that your employer will not take it well – you will be seriously stressed and unfortunately that is too often the result. A neighbour of mine worked as a salesman and was a successful, hardworking employee, always achieving his targets and making money for the firm. However, when a colleague left, forcing him to do the job of two people with the same pay and with much unpleasantness from his boss, he suffered a nervous breakdown and all that goes with it. He was absent from work for many months and the firm had a very difficult problem to deal with. A bit of help and understanding would have led to a much better outcome from all concerned. The firm learnt the hard way.

In my teaching, being understanding is key. Yes, there are standards to uphold, rules to respect and we need to teach children to produce their best as often as they can, but my goodness, as teachers, we have to show understanding on plenty of occasions! Students can be tired in a lesson after spending the previous evening rehearsing for the school play or travelling back from a sports match or a concert. They may not have been able to do homework for a perfectly good reason or achieved a low mark in a test because they were absent when it was set, had a family issue or had been ill. There are always many situations each term when I have to use my judgement to determine whether a student is swinging the lead or whether I need to accept their explanation. It becomes easier to spot these things with experience!

Understanding

In today's world, so much hate and suffering would be avoided if people showed a little more understanding for cultural differences and appreciated each other's customs and values more fully. In Britain, we are pretty good at this compared to some, it has to be said, but this is not the case everywhere. It is so sad that this lack of understanding is at the root of so many wars and conflicts between people around the world. However, we have made great strides in how we help people who are in some way disadvantaged or handicapped. We could do more, but much has been achieved in recent years and their profile has been raised in so many ways. In schools, there is far more help for dyslexics and dyspraxics, for example, and staff are trained to appreciate the difficulties they face and how they can help them to overcome them and reach their potential. Equally, for people who are physically handicapped, there is now a far greater awareness of the daily challenges they face and a greater appreciation of the tremendous efforts they make to be successful in life despite their handicaps.

All that said, we still have a way to go and your generation is, in my estimation, really well placed to carry the banner and make the world that much better through being more understanding and aware of challenges that people face. This is all the more remarkable as some of your present role models in world politics do not cover themselves in glory in this regard. Happily, you three and many of your generation recognise this, and I do hope that the world will not have suffered too much from the ravages of the present generation of world leaders and will leave you all with the ability to protect the planet and bring greater peace and understanding to it in the years to come. I must say that despite what is happening, I have great confidence in you all and in those of future generations. Good luck!

V

is for

VALOUR

> *"The Lord is with thee,
> thou mighty man of valour."*

Judges, ch6 v12 (spoken to Gideon)

VALOUR

Valour is such a great word. We think of John Bunyan and 'He who would valiant be, 'gainst all disaster'. We think of knights of old in jousting tournaments, we think of soldiers on the battlefield, we think of amazing acts of heroism, we think, of course, of the Victoria Cross and its motto – For Valour. It is such an evocative word, yet here I am going to try and connect it with your lives. You will at times, however cosy and sheltered your lives may be (and I doubt that is what you have in mind!), need to have recourse to a bit of valour to get you through. I hope, of course, that this need will not trouble you often, but life has the capacity to lay a few snares around to trip you up and cause you harm or distress. I sincerely hope not, but remember my earlier motto: "Be prepared!"

What will assist you will certainly be an element of preparation as I have suggested, but you will need to delve down and find that courage, that inner strength, that valour to get out of that challenging or tricky situation. Most of us have difficult days at work, in relationships, in dealing with awkward people, in coping with illness or lack of money and these can understandably cause stress and lead you to feel very low. But don't let them! Don't let the bad things in life get you down and defeat you. Most of the time, things will be good – I sincerely believe that – but inevitably, there will be problems and you will need to keep your chin up and go into battle. However, if you do find yourselves in difficulty, I know it may be a challenge, but try to stay dignified. It can be natural to seek revenge and lash out, but you don't go there. When it is all over, your conscience will be clearer and you will feel that much happier for having kept the moral high ground and for not having succumbed to the levels of those who wish you harm and discomfort. Believe me, when you look back you will be glad you acted that way.

I had a tough year over a decade ago and it was a time when I sincerely felt that I had made some daft moves and I was heading towards a disaster of my own making. Thankfully, I got through it, made some good decisions, talked to people who helped and prayed – many a time! I have scarcely mentioned faith, but I have to say that it has been my rock through difficult times and some incredibly positive things have happened that I can only put down to the benevolent intervention of the Almighty. How I managed to end up in the wonderful school that I am at is itself a real blessing and that came after suffering some challenging days. When I have bad days now and again, I think back to those days and can only say, "Wow!" at getting from there to here. Even in the darkest moments, if you keep believing and stay courageous, amazing things can happen.

I saw a television interview with the actor Michael Caine many years ago and with the passage of time, I remember little of it. I do recall his hatred of impressionists and his version of 'My name is Michael Caine – not a lot of people know that!' still brings a smile – I can't convey it on paper, but believe me, it was funny! I also recall him talking about some of the hardships of his childhood years and his father saying how important it was to learn from the bad times – to use them. You may not enjoy them, but once you are through them, they are certainly character building. I also remember a former student who was at university studying creative writing. He was attending the most prestigious course in the country at the time and was thoroughly enjoying it. However, he considered that he was way off being able to craft a novel. The reason? Quite simply, he said (with much laughter) that life had, at that point, been too kind to him. Not enough bad things had happened to make him creative! I can't say that my own motivation to write would rest on that, but that's what he claimed. My sincere hope is that he has yet to start writing!

W

is for

WORK

> *"It's true hard work never killed anybody, but I figure why take the chance?"*
>
> Ronald Reagan

WORK

In the future, will you work to live or live to work? Well, considering how much time you spend at work and the fact that your job inevitably defines you in some way, you will end up somewhere in between. As teachers, we often veer towards the latter as we take so much work home with us and our proper experience of living seems to take place in the holidays. Maybe that's rather a bleak view, but then in teaching the grass never seems green enough – not to put you off teaching, by the way! The reality is that many jobs demand a lot these days and this, coupled with the commute, can make working life a drudge, especially if the job itself is not to your liking.

So what's the answer; how should you approach your working life to get the most from it? I would answer quite simply by saying that you should choose a line of work that you enjoy, something that enthuses you whenever you think about it and makes you want to jump out of bed in the morning and look forward to the day. If it pays well, people don't take advantage of you, colleagues are nice and the commute is small, then that's perfect. I'd also add that you may well find that the location of your place of work is quite a big factor – it certainly has been with me. One of the big advantages of being a teacher is that you can more easily select which area of the country that you would like to work in. As I have grown older, this has become a more important factor for me personally, but for many, it's not an issue at all. However, what is vital is enjoyment of what you do. This may not always be possible, but if you have a clear goal in mind and a definite idea of what you would like to be, then the sooner you can set yourself on the road to that promised land.

Pleasingly, all of you understand the importance of work experience in your teenage years and two of you have already had part-time jobs, which have prepared you in many ways for the demands of the workplace. You have learnt the importance of customer relations, keeping up standards, timekeeping, getting along with colleagues and how to pace yourself through long shifts among many other things. We are really proud of you for coping so well in the workplace at such a young age and the hours that you have spent doing some quite challenging tasks will undoubtedly stand you in good stead once you start looking for full-time employment after you have finished your studies in the years to come. You have also gained a greater appreciation of money, which is so important at a young age – you really have to respect it!

Now I have used the word 'jobs' rather a lot so far and I will now switch to the rather grander term of 'career'. Yes, parents generally want their children to look to pursue a skill or career as these form the basis of financial security and we are no different. I would not want to push you into any direction in life as such immense choices are yours alone. You will make your own decisions and, dare I say it, your own mistakes. That said, one of the reasons for writing is to help you not to make too many of these. As a parent, I want you to learn from *my* mistakes and not repeat them. I am certainly not saying that teaching was a mistake for me, but in today's world, teaching is, if anything, a harder profession to succeed in than it was thirty years ago when I was considering my options. Saying that, it's never been dull, most of my colleagues and students have been wonderful and I have not been poorly paid. I have had some great experiences and have had the real joy of being able to teach you all and share, for a short period of time, your exciting educational journeys. Amazingly your mother has been there too, and we will always be grateful for that experience.

When I started in the workplace, the belief was that you would set yourself up for the one major career which would sustain you until retirement. Whilst that is still largely true and you have to start out young to work up the ladder, there is a case for having more than one career in a working lifetime and I certainly considered that at one stage. There is no shame if you do and varying your experience of work can be really refreshing and reinvigorating. I took a career break when I reached forty and although I returned to the same career thereafter, the change pressed the reset button, so to speak, and was no bad thing. As to what it is you will do and when you will choose to do it, that has to be up to you. I was once told that if in any doubt as to how to proceed in such matters, listen to your gut. It will tell you how you really feel and whether the move is right for you. I have to say that when I have done this, it has unquestionably led to the right decision, but when, for whatever reason, I have chosen to ignore it, it has ended up causing me bitter regret. My message, therefore, is quite simple – you *will* find that right career path in the end, but you may need to be honest with yourself and wrestle with your inner feelings first. Trust me, if you do that, you will all be fine and really do something great with your lives.

X

is for

XMAS

"I will honour Christmas in my heart, and try to keep it all the year"

Charles Dickens (*A Christmas Carol*, 1843)

XMAS

Now, where would we be without Christmas?! Its appearance in the depths of dark, cold winters is just vital for so many of our lives and the months leading up to it are laden with ever-increasing excitement, colour and song. Well, that's how it should be in an ideal world. The fact that it leads to fractious family arguments, burdensome debt and profound loneliness for those who have no loved ones is the other side, and one that we must not ignore. It is also one of those things that creep up on you and you cannot ignore. There will be expensive Christmas shopping, an over-indulgence in the worst kind of food and drink, repeats of ancient TV specials and constant renditions of the same carols and Christmas pop songs, to name but few. If you want to be a scrooge and complain about Christmas, you can, and you can start complaining in late August when shops seem to start preparing for it!

As you will know, my view is rather different. I have always loved so much about it and it has always served to remind me how fortunate I am. So many of my happiest family memories stem from Christmas and I never tire of talking about them. It always reminds me of Christmas Days with my grandparents in Coventry, squeezing round a couple of tables joined together and filled high with a variety of meats, vegetables, condiments and wine – yes, the good old Hock and Blue Nun. As everyone did in those days, the decorations were up long before and added so much colour and fun to the occasion for us youngsters – as did the crackers. It never mattered how good the little gifts were or if the paper hats happened to split. We just got on with it and enjoyed the occasion. I can well remember piling my plate and never managing to finish all of the first course, but still amazingly always finding a bit of room somewhere for the essential trifle or pudding. The opening of presents and the appearance of games always followed the food and none of us youngsters could wait – it was always a magical time. Unsurprisingly, much of this is incorporated into our own Christmases today – though the wine has improved in quality, even if the cracker jokes have not.

However, nowadays there seem to be even more compulsory aspects to that Christmas meal: we need those Christmas sweaters, we need those mobile phones for the selfies and for the conversations with those who cannot make it and we need to have better crackers for the slightly less rubbishy gifts. Still, I can live with all that as they all make it more fun and therefore more memorable. I doubt we're alone here, but we absolutely have to cover the puddings with brandy and set fire to them or it just wouldn't be Christmas – and everything has to stop for the Queen at 3pm. To be honest, as parents, it has not escaped our notice that we have very much imposed our idea of Christmas on you. There are, indeed, certain things that we have introduced as new traditions because we have taken the best things that we remember from our childhood. I have talked about some of mine, but we also have the pasta course as the first course – a legacy from your mother's Italian background, and we feel that it's important not to lose the religious aspect, so we go to church and unashamedly have carols playing so much of the time – much to your annoyance, we know. However, you will yourselves choose what you want to continue from what we do (and this will hopefully be a lot!) and will doubtless add new aspects. We look forward to that!

It has to be said that Christmas really is a time for counting your blessings, never mind how long you have to queue for things or how much cash you have to part with at the checkouts. As I said, the memories are priceless and help to bind the family together so wonderfully – the fact that we in effect have three meals – as we have two other Christmas dinners with others in the family between then and New Year – is fantastic. We can't get enough of it all!

At the same time, it always amazes me how well we as a nation try to look after people at Christmas. The amount of time that some people devote voluntarily to charity work can be staggering and it makes such a difference to those who are in less fortunate circumstances. Some activities such as carol-singing can be great fun, but I take my hat off to people who stand for hours on end on freezing street corners rattling tins or who visit sick people in hospital or work jolly hard to cook and dish out meals to the homeless. I really admire such people and gladly part with a bit of cash here and there to help make their efforts worthwhile. There's the true spirit of Christmas!

I have to finish with a word about the religious aspect that many a vicar implores us never to forget as we tuck in to the turkey and trimmings. As I grew up in a very Christian primary school, this went hand in hand with the build-up to Christmas and we were soon very familiar with the Christmas story. It is certainly important that we do not lose sight of why it's all happening; the fact that we are all celebrating the birth over two thousand years ago of someone very special. And let's face it, the mere fact that we do celebrate it so well is testament to the immense influence that Jesus continues to have on our lives all this time later. In this increasing secular world and despite all the kitsch and gluttony, it does help to keep the Christian message strong and alive and hopefully this will not diminish in your lifetimes.

Y

is for

YOUTHFULNESS

"Youth is the one thing worth having."

Oscar Wilde (*The Picture of Dorian Gray*, 1890)

YOUTHFULNESS

The quest for youthfulness and corresponding good health has always been a part of the human psyche. Most of us do not relish the ageing process and do what we can to hold it back. However, even the fittest of us have to succumb one day and the hard task that faces you as you get older is that you have to get on the treadmill and undergo some serious pain just to function adequately. Now, apart from the weekly run, the occasional cycle ride and the odd attendance at a gym, I have failed miserably in this endeavour and know that I will have to improve sharpish – mañana will not be enough. Like many of my generation, I have struggled to find the time I need to properly maintain my fitness, but when I do exercise, I notice the difference – and always think how fit I would be if I had exercised effectively since university. You, however, can still do that and in doing so, you will doubtless feel the benefits well into your retirement years (assuming that retirement will still happen for your generation!). I am still clinging onto the hope that I will be able to emulate my grandad and be climbing high hills energetically well into my eighties – some hope, that!

As parents, we want you to have long, happy lives and to live to see generations after you prosper and make their own mark on the world. To do this, diet, exercise and lifestyle choices will make the difference. As I am suggesting, do not take my example, but follow the healthier trends of your own generation and keep looking to stay fit. We have always tried to provide healthy meals for you and to have as much fresh fruit and vegetables around for you to enjoy. You have all certainly grasped the importance of this and have a good attitude, but please keep this going through the less financially stable periods of your life. It may not be easy, but it is very much the case that you are what you eat and eating plenty of the right stuff will make your lives easier in the long run. The aim has to be to have plenty of foods that fill you with energy and help your body to function well. I would also urge you to remember the importance of sleep. Now I know that I am a fine one to talk, suffering as I do from our genetic predisposition to be night owls, but it is so important. Try also to either join a gym or invest in one for home as again, finding opportunities to exercise in busy life schedules is a problem, and please strive to do better than me! I fancy, though, that such will be the advancements in medicine and sports science in your lifetimes that you will be helped considerably by professional advice in ways that our generation were not. Both my PE teachers at school smoked cigarettes – and quite openly – and other sports staff were significantly overweight, so the role models were not there for us, although on our last day, our headmaster did tell us to beware the pot belly that comes with too many business lunches!

Other Things:

1. Be around positive people, as they will keep you young, happy and refreshed.
2. Laugh every day – laugh out loud and keep that smile active or you'll lose it. As you have all got great smiles, we don't want that!
3. Share jokes and humour with those around you, especially family. It relaxes and makes you feel that much happier – even if you are the butt of such jokes as I often am!
4. Look after your senses. Life is so rich when all are working well.
5. Go on regular walks in the country. Breathe in the fresh air and feel glad to be alive.
6. Master a sport or two – at least one which you can play socially and one which may be more solitary.
7. Avoid spending too much time in front of a screen.
8. Don't be afraid to go to the doctor ever – catching problems early saves lives.
9. Go on regular holidays and breaks to have a proper rest.
10. Above all, stay young inside. Be silly occasionally. Make a fool of yourself now and then. Don't be afraid to laugh at yourself. I do it all the time – it helps keep me sane!

Z

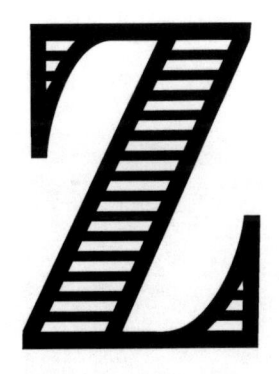

is for

ZEST

"If you have zest and enthusiasm, you attract zest and enthusiasm."

Norman Vincent Peale

ZEST

Zest is a great word. My trusty Penguin dictionary defines it as 'keen enjoyment, gusto' and for me, this is how you must aim to approach life and all the major things that you do. Some people are said to have a real 'zest for life', intending to make the most of everything and making that really clear. Linked to this, I would argue, is the ability to have a sense of wonder at things around them, whether natural or man-made and to be able to see the good and the potential in others. Essentially, by being open to such things and looking for the positives, you will enhance your own pleasure and elation, building up that all-important zest factor.

Now you might think that I am just going to jump on the bandwagon here and say that enjoying life and approaching it with enthusiasm means that you cannot do this alone at any point, but I would say quite the opposite. Leave a space for yourself each day. Put some time aside for yourself and reinvigorate yourself by doing a bit of what you fancy and reflect on the good things in the day. You haven't even got to do anything in particular – just spend some time recharging and realigning that zest that you need for another great day. As you know, I like my cappuccino breaks and these are my reinvigorating times. I sip a capp and can be alone in my thoughts and reflections. I like to choose somewhere nice to have it as that kind of location gives me that positive, thankful vibe that I need. Make sure you have that moment too!

Having a zest for life also means enjoying the experience of life and not letting bad things get you down. It means celebrating achievements, having a party, listening to great music, singing songs, playing instruments, watching films and so on and so on. It means that, of course, but having a zest for life also means taking care of your own life too. If you do that, you will have more and more of it to enjoy and be able to spread your positive glow around to light up so many lives. You owe it to yourself and everyone else in your family to do your best to stay safe – yes, to stay alive. You have already done so much in your lives and touched those of so many people and you owe it to them to take care and not take unnecessary risks. Please always be sensible about driving, drinking, safe sex, dangerous sports and guarding yourself against crime in all its forms.

The world is a wonderful place, but it's not safe – there are dangers every day. I'm not saying that you shouldn't do some parachuting or kayaking down rapids, but be very careful about your own safety. Your mother and I knew a splendid young man when we were in our twenties. He was a student first at my school and then at your mother's. He was a great character, the life and soul of every party, immensely popular with his peers, yet equally charming and engaging with adults too. He had a real zest for life unquestionably, but in one respect he sadly lowered his guard, drank a little too much one evening, fell asleep in his car and never woke up. It was such a tragedy. I think also of people I know who have been badly injured or killed in road traffic accidents. Vehicles are dangerous things, and a moment's loss of concentration can be fatal. Never get into a car with someone who has been drinking – period – or indeed, anyone who likes to show off by driving recklessly, as some young people sadly do. I have to say these things as my parents have said the same to me and you will surely say the same to your own children. Please look after yourselves. It means that you are responsible and care about those close to you too – for whom your lives mean so much.

As parents we know that we will have to let you make your own decisions in so many things from now on; we will have to let go, and that can be a frightening prospect, as we fifty-somethings know of so many of the snares and dangers and want you to avoid them – that's one reason for me writing this for all of you. However, as I said way back in the introduction, you are all wonderfully sensible and will, I am sure, take all my ramblings in the right way and I hope that what I have done is made clear what I think are the most important things to carry with you on this incredible journey through life. I hope that it will be everything that you want it to be and that in your later days, when you look back on where you been and what you have achieved, you will look back with so much pride and satisfaction and will, in turn, pass on what you see as important to your own special ones.

Enjoy the ride! xxx

BIBLIOGRAPHY

Bridget Grenville-Cleave : *Positive Psychology: A toolkit for happiness, purpose and well-being* : Icon Books Ltd; 2012; 119–125

Collins Book of Quotations: Harper Collins; 2013:

1. Ambition: "The Gospel of Getting On." George Bernard Shaw (*Mrs Warren's Profession*, 1898)
2. Education: "I pay the schoolmaster, but 'tis the schoolboys that educate my son." Ralph Waldo Emerson (Journals)
3. Family: "Treasure your families – the future of humanity passes by way of the family." John Paul II (Speech, 1982)
4. Hope: "He that lives in hope danceth without music." George Herbert (*Jacula Prudentum*, 1640)

5. Kindness: "So many gods, so many creeds / So many paths that wind and wind, / While the art of being kind / Is all the sad world needs." Ella Wheeler Wilcox (*The World's Need*, 1917)

6. Money: "And money is like muck, not good except it be spread." Francis Bacon (*Of Seditions and Troubles*, 1625)

7. Nature: "All my life through, the new sights of Nature made me rejoice like a child." Marie Curie (Pierre Curie)

8. Time: "I wasted time, and now doth time waste me." William Shakespeare (*Richard II, 1597*)

9. Work: "It's true hard work never killed anybody, but I figure why take the chance?" Ronald Reagan

Oxford Dictionary of Quotations (ed. Knowles): Oxford University Press; 2004:

1. Ambition: "Ah, but a man's reach should exceed his grasp, / Or what's a heaven for?" Robert Browning (*Andrea del Sarto*, 1855)

2. Broadmindedness: "The superior man is broadminded." Confucius (*Analects*, ch2 v14)

Bibliography

3. Gratitude: "A joy and pleasant thing it is to be thankful." The Book of Common Prayer (Psalm 147:1)

4. Interests: "All intellectual improvement arises from leisure." James Boswell (*The Life of Samuel Johnson*, 1791) Joy: "Joy, beautiful radiance of the gods." Friedrich von Schiller (*An die Freude*, 1785)

5. Love: "There is only one happiness in life, to love and be loved." George Sand (*Letter to Lina Calamatta*, 1862)

6. Preparation: "Be prepared." Robert Baden-Powell (*Scouting for Boys*, 1908)

7. Sensitivity: "I shook the habit off / Entirely and for ever, and again / In Nature's presence stood, as now I stand, /A sensitive being, a *creative* soul." William Wordsworth (*The Prelude*, 1850)

8. Understanding: "I shall light a candle of understanding in thine heart, which shall not be put out." Apocrypha (II Esdras, ch14 v25)

9. Valour: "The Lord is with thee, thou mighty man of valour." Judges, ch6 v12 (spoken to Gideon)

Barack Obama – 2008 Presidential Campaign "Yes We Can"

The Penguin English Dictionary: Penguin Books; 1986

Chris Williams: *The Richard Burton Diaries*: Yale; 2012

www.brainyquote.com

1. Reflection: "I love the man that can smile in trouble, that can gather strength from distress, and grow brave by reflection." Thomas Paine
2. Zest: "If you have zest and enthusiasm, you attract zest and enthusiasm." Norman Vincent Peale

www.businessinsider.com

1. Questioning: "The important thing is not to stop questioning. Curiosity has its own reason for existing." Albert Einstein

www.goodreads.com

1. Creativity: "Odd how the creative power at once brings the whole universe to order." Virginia Woolf

2. Xmas: "I will honour Christmas in my heart, and try to keep it all the year." Charles Dickens (*A Christmas Carol*, 1843)
3. Youthfulness: "Youth is the one thing worth having." Oscar Wilde (*The Picture of Dorian Gray*, 1890)

www.wiseoldsayings.com

1. "Insist upon yourself. Be original." Ralph Waldo Emerson

And finally…

A big thank you to my dear friend John Hunt, who sadly passed away in April 2019, but whose advice and encouragement set me on the path to producing this book.